Country Girl
to City Girl

FINDING MY PATH

By Leslie Killian Greenlee

Team WV Press
Philadelphia, PA
www.teamWVpress.com

The author alone is responsible for statements of fact, opinions, recommendations, and conclusions expressed. The publication in no way implies approval or expresses the opinions of TeamWV Press.

In accordance with the 55 Copyright Act of 1976, the scanning, uploading, and electronic sharing of any part of this book without the permission of the publisher constitute unlawful piracy and theft of intellectual property. **Please purchase only authorized electronic editions of this work and do not encourage piracy of copyrighted materials.** If you would like to use material from the book, prior written permission must be obtained. Please contact the publisher at www.teamWVpress.com/permissions

Country Girl to City Girl. Finding my Path. Copyright © 2023 by Leslie Killian Greenlee.

All rights reserved.

ISBN: 9798858076940

This book may be purchased at www.teamWVpress.com

First Edition: 2023

Book Design by: Sueli Vieira

Dedication

This book is a tribute to my mother, who left us too soon but continues to live on inside of me. She inspired me to live life to the fullest and motivated me to work hard to succeed in everything I do. I want to thank you for all of your help as I was growing up. I appreciate you reminding me of the most crucial aspects of life. Mother, I love you.

Acknowledgments

I owe much thanks to my publishing family. First and foremost, I wish to thank my editors, Norma Wingate and Sueli Vieira, who were very instrumental in this process.

I'd like to extend my sincere gratitude to Bill, my husband, and my wonderful friends Mary and Leslie for their insightful comments on the text's structure. I value your friendship and assistance. My sincere gratitude and appreciation to the Team WV Press team for their support and for doing what they do so expertly on my behalf. Please accept my sincere gratitude to both Sueli and Norma.

Foreword

We, as the editors of this project, are honored to provide a platform for Leslie Killian Greenlee to share her insights and viewpoints. We deeply appreciate her choice of a female minority-owned publishing house, showcasing her commitment to fostering diverse voices. Having been a supporter of previous authors, Leslie now steps into the spotlight to publish her own book.

Our association with Leslie Greenlee dates back to 2017 when we first crossed paths on the tennis courts of 33rd Street in Philadelphia. Our interactions have been marked by fierce competition, both in 3.5 singles and 7.0 doubles. A relentless spirit, Leslie fearlessly embraces challenges, and her reputation for unwavering determination is widespread throughout the Philly area. Her small stature belies a powerful forehand that her opponents have come to know all too well.

This same tenacious approach defines her journey with this book. Leslie's abiding desire for success, coupled with her commitment to seeing those around her flourish, is evident in her endeavor. By penning this book on work ethic, she extends her drive to empower others. The pages of her book offer a window into Mrs. Greenlee's life, recounting her experiences, travels, education, and passions. She then equips readers with practical techniques derived from real-world scenarios, aiding them in their quest for personal growth.

With her debut work, "Country Girl to City Girl. Finding my Path," Leslie Killian Greenlee bares her vulnerability, shares her unfiltered honesty, and sprinkles in her characteristic wit. We are truly proud to present this book to readers, confident that its insights will resonate and inspire. Here's to embarking on a journey of growth and happiness through these pages.

Team WV Press, Editors

Norma Wingate & Sueli Vieira

Content

Country Girl to City Girl. Finding my Path. 1
Family 3
Mother 4
Father 7
Maryanne - Father's Wife 10
Bill - Husband 11
Early Life Experiences 15
Growing Up In A Small Town 15
Business In A Small Town 17
The Farms 19
Education: Reality vs Expectations 21
Private College - Albright College 21
Public University - Temple University 23
Public University - Grad School - West Chester University 24
Personal Interests: The Escape 27
Tennis - A Community 27
Jazz - More Than a Genre of Music 29
Traveling The Globe 31
Morocco 33

Japan	36
Saudi Arabia	37
The Work Ethic of People in Varied Businesses	**41**
Food Stand at Farmer's Market	42
Biologist in a Laboratory	44
Construction Workers From Other Countries	45
Local Bartender	46
Local Dry Cleaners	48
Owner, Local Bagel Restaurant	49
Local Food Store	51
Owner, Local Diner	51
Work Ethic in Academia and Community Service	**55**
Friend, a Professor	55
Professor Number Two	56
College Supervisor	57
Supervisor at a Non-Profit	59
Witnessing Students' Work Ethics	**61**
Student Interactions	61
A Determined Student, Non-Profit	62
Special Student	64
Incorporating Work Ethic In The Real World	**67**
About the Author	**71**

Country Girl to City Girl. Finding my Path.

Leslie believes work ethic can be like a roller coaster where a person can flip back and forth throughout their life. It has to do with how a person is raised and how the work experience is emphasized. People have different ideas about this aspect of life depending on whether their parents worked or not, and what kind of work they were involved in. The work ethic also has to do with how much parents pushed their children to do well in life, and how their children received this. It also involves how much love the parents contributed, and how the children interpreted this. Was there enough time that the parents spent with their children to emphasize the importance of work ethic? How did the children perceive the parents' lifestyle relating to their work experience? The work ethic also pertains to what the children perceive after relating to their neighbors, friends, and relatives.

Leslie's philosophy of work is to be able to pursue your potential in any environment and to be happy with your success. She admits that sometimes she was not at the top of her game because of a crazy supervisor, or a soap opera atmosphere, but she moved on to the next level as a professional because of her unstoppable motivation. 'She can always get up when she is pushed far down.'

For a good work ethic, Leslie says that you must be the best manager, of course, with your own work. Gossiping is not helpful when you must respect others at your job. Don't get into that trap! Your co-workers are not your friends. If you are interested and capable, move up the ladder to another management level. Throughout your journey, you should work well with your colleagues and perform well with teamwork.

Family

Leslie grew up in Fleetwood, a small town in Pennsylvania surrounded by small farms owned by Mennonites and Pennsylvania Dutch people (Descended from Germany). The closest major city was Reading, thirty minutes away, with about 200,000 inhabitants.

The land around the town housed mostly dairy farms that were operated by less than five people. The town of Fleetwood had small businesses that were necessary to assist a population of approximately 3000 people. Some of these businesses consisted of a bank, a grocery store, a mini-market, a hardware store, a meat market, a pharmacy, an insurance company, sandwich shops, a few bars, gas stations, a tannery, a cookie factory, etc. The people were real friendly because everyone knew a lot of people in the town. They had lived there for many years and may have also worked there. They were simple folks who didn't earn a lot of money and seemed content with the small town atmosphere.

Leslie was raised in a household with four siblings that had various struggles because of family dynamics. Sometimes it felt like they were in a zoo with all of the crazy emotional ups and downs. As a result of the work ethic in the house, with a father that was a family doctor, a mother that was a nurse, and with the influence of the people in the small town they grew up, the four brothers and sisters learned that the work ethic is necessary and essential to bring happiness and success. They understood from the small businesses in the area, along with their father's practice, that you must have a good work ethic to survive in life. There was no choice but to put up with the rules and structure.

Mother

Leslie's mother grew up working class, married a doctor, and was able to travel the world while raising five children. She contracted Parkinson's Disease when she was 38 years old, but always had a positive frame of mind with no sign of complaints. At the time, there was a thought that she acquired this disease possibly from an insect bite in Africa, or possibly

Rheumatic Fever. She drank a sip of blackberry brandy every day to calm her nerves.

    Her mother had a different work ethic to maintain her own health, and this was demonstrated to her children through the meaning of determination. She also worked as a nurse in her husband's doctor's practice in the house while running back and forth to raise her children. Later in life after all the children left to move on with their lives, Leslie's grandmother helped to take care of her mother, which was an amazing task for an 80 year old woman.

    Some of her amazing experiences and talents included traveling to Africa, India, China and other parts of the world. When she was in Africa, she was in charge of all the cameras by carrying them on her shoulder, for example; a day camera, night camera, movie camera. As a result of this journey, she understood the significance of good pictures. In her free time, she painted still life pictures with oil paints which were, of course,

spread all over the house. Her cooking involved, definitely, the typical Irish dish, Shepherd's pie because of her Irish blood, the string bean casserole and the pressure cooker beef stew, among others. She was a king of the casseroles. Her signature cake was the typical pound cake with no icing which was a favorite of the children growing up. Even though she liked to cook, she wasn't in any way a gourmet chef. For sewing, she loved to take Vogue patterns and adjust them to create her own fashions.

The family misses her for her gorgeous looks along with the classy outfits that she wore. Her Parkinson's Disease took her away from the family too early, but they often think about her warmth and great inspiration to live a life to their potential.

Father

Leslie's father was a general practice family doctor with a home office. As a physician, he had a good work ethic because he serviced patients from all walks of life and treated anything from a common cold to many more severe diseases. Her father understood that each patient had their own idea of what an emergency encompassed, so he had to attend to each case differently. Many times he worked until 10 PM at night to handle all kinds of medical issues. Her father even handed out free medicine for common ailments to make it easier for patients.

One time during the middle of the night, Leslie almost experienced a baby delivery that he performed at a local farm of Mennonites. What kind of an experience this would have been, but on that day Leslie was feeling under the weather and was not able to go along with her father. This would have been a 'one and only' experience for her.

As a child, it was fun when the patients brought Leslie's father home-made sweets such as; shoe fly pie (It isn't as it sounds), peach pie, Pennsylvania Dutch meatloaf ('With everything, but the kitchen sink'), knitted clothing, or other gifts to show their appreciation. They were passionate about their cooking and other creations. You would think this would have been ingrained in Leslie's upbringing for the long haul. She tried to hand-make things for a while, but then the interest for computers took over.

Leslie's father was also Mr. Fixit around the house with many projects going on at once, such as; fixing a hole in the floor, repairing the roof, painting a room, re-finishing floors, installing pipes, and planting trees. (Sorry, but 'he didn't fix potholes!') He didn't believe in hiring anyone if he could repair it himself.

Twenty minutes from their house, they had a cabin, which they called the summer home where they'd go spend their weekends. As a way to teach his children work ethic, he made them install pipes in the ground and put on a new roof at the cabin. During this time, the children were not allowed to play with their friends. They were 'glued to the cabin' as work assistants. Oh well, 'it was quite an experience.'

Another project instilled in the siblings by Leslie's father was to plant a million trees ('Not literally') every summer. One summer, the children had to plant 25 trees, but when a storm appeared, they had to continue the process until they were finished. As a result of this, the next day, Leslie acquired pneumonia which was grueling and had to attend school the next day, anyway. That was the end of her desire to plant trees.

Leslie's father's work ethic did not stop at these two things. He was also an accomplished jazz musician who wrote music and performed in a band. He believed that practice makes perfect. Leslie's father practiced for an hour or two every night which he considered necessary in order to succeed. He influenced his children with jazz music and engaging in the playing of instruments. Her father emphasized that you must practice every day to move to another level.

There were many instruments in the house, various saxophones, a drum set, vibraphone, clarinet, violin, flute, piccolo, and a piano. Leslie's father set his children up to play either the clarinet, saxophone, or flute along with the piano. The siblings didn't have a choice as far as what instrument they would play. He felt that the clarinet, saxophone, and flute were versatile enough that they could be played in different kinds of bands.

To this day, the two older children are still playing jazz with the clarinet, saxophone, and piano, and practicing every day. The demanding energy that it takes to practice daily will pay off. ('Trust me!')

Maryanne - Father's Wife

According to Leslie, Maryanne has a great work ethic in handling a farm life and caring for various animals whether they were her own, or stray animals. As a child, she worked tirelessly participating in horse competitions in Philadelphia and other local areas. Along with this, she had to take care of the health of the horses with baths, horseshoes, etc.

She was never afraid of work. Stray cats would arrive on her porch, and she'd immediately name all of them with really slick names (Slippers, Spud, Tiny, Meatball), and fed them three times a day. At one time, she had up to 30 stray cats. Maryanne treats these animals as though they are her own and a part of the family. In addition, she helped build cat houses on the porch. One of the stray cats had an eye problem and she got medical treatment for her. She owns one cat that lives in her house that she named, 'Tiny.'

When Maryanne married Leslie's father, she put a lot of energy into repairing the farmhouse, whether it was painting the rooms, cleaning the snow off the roof, peeling off the wallpaper, tarring the roof, mowing the seven-acre land, etc.

Bill - Husband

For over three decades, Leslie noticed that Bill has been a beacon of unwavering work ethic, a steadfast presence in the realm of local politics in Philadelphia. His indefatigable energy has been an enduring force, shaping his legacy as a stalwart advocate for change and a champion of the people. From voter registration drives to aiding individuals across the socioeconomic spectrum and endorsing aspiring candidates, Bill's tireless commitment has left an indelible mark.

Bill's journey commenced as a committee person, a district representative within a ward spanning several city blocks. From the very moment Leslie crossed paths with him, Bill's fervent dedication to the neighborhood became evident. Be it potholes, voter registration, or bus routes, his unwavering concern encompassed the minutiae that constitutes community life. His altruism was unassailable; bribery was a foreign concept, and his doors were open to all, irrespective of their political affiliation. Bill was a vanguard for voter enfranchisement, creating informative letters outlining candidates and gracing polling stations on election day to champion his endorsed contenders. This conscientious stewardship solidified his standing as an electable force, with a follow-up prowess akin to drawing a straight line.

Progressing from committee person to Assistant to a Councilman, Bill's realm expanded, and his commitment to constituents remained tireless. His relentless dedication transformed him into the epitome of a public servant, a rock star who didn't take center stage but shone brightly when needed. His ascent continued, leading him to the role of Ward Leader, a coveted position among the city's 69 wards. In this intricate dance of politics, Bill exhibited a unique ability to traverse diverse walks of life, navigating a circus-like environment of ward leaders, each with their own intricate choreography of demands and expectations. The art of communication became Bill's forte, a skillful tightrope walk that balanced egos, neighborhood issues, and financial considerations, all while nurturing a network of connections that solidified his stature.

Bill's political odyssey was a symphony of connection, harmonizing with individuals of all backgrounds. While political allegiances often draw stark lines, Bill transcended divisions, forming connections that resonated far beyond the sphere of mere politics. Yet, his journey wasn't a steady march but a rollercoaster ride, navigating the daily challenges of constituents and ward leaders alike, each interaction laden with potential highs and lows. His role demanded resilience, from addressing emotionally charged visitors to defusing confrontations with self-centered critics. Bill's unique perch within the Councilman's office forged powerful alliances, driving change through impactful legislation, touching lives with tangible reforms.

Navigating the labyrinth of negotiation, Bill's prowess came to the fore. His artful ability to foster relationships and orchestrate consensus led him to be sought out by fellow council members and even the Council President. He was a friend to all, adept at reconciling competing interests and steering the ship of politics through turbulent waters. His dedication to the craft was evident in his tenacity, tirelessly shuttling back and forth, a masterful dance to propel bills towards fruition. For Bill, this was the very essence of political work ethic, an ethos that went beyond personal ego and aimed at achieving a collective vision.

Bill's journey wasn't without its challenges, navigating a landscape where the term "politician" carries connotations both inspiring and disparaging. Yet, he defied this dichotomy, embodying the role with integrity and effectiveness. His determination was exemplified when he ran for Councilman's seat in a Special Election, winning resoundingly. His commitment expanded, amplifying his advocacy for women's rights, as he championed crucial issues such as paid sick leave and salary fairness.

In the annals of Philadelphia's political tapestry, Bill's legacy shines as a testament to the power of tireless dedication, the art of compromise, and the unyielding pursuit of betterment. His narrative echoes a refrain of service, echoing through the corridors of power, embodying the nuanced dance of a politician who stands not for ego but for the people, not for division but for consensus. Bill's work ethic is a symphony of integrity, resilience, and dedication, an enduring melody that resonates as a beacon for all who seek to serve and uplift.

Early Life Experiences

Growing Up In A Small Town

Growing up in the embrace of a quaint small town, Leslie was instilled with an invaluable lesson: a robust work ethic isn't just a choice; it's an integral facet of life itself. The notion of half-hearted efforts found no foothold in her upbringing; instead, she imbibed the essence of commitment, always striving for excellence in her chosen pursuits. The path to progress was illuminated by the pursuit of education and the cultivation of harmonious relationships with colleagues. Indeed, the key to unlocking success in both career and life lay in the realm of effective communication.

Within the life aspects of small-town existence, Leslie also mastered the art of independence. She embraced challenges head-on, adroitly tackling household repairs and refusing to rely solely on others within her professional realm. This sense of self-reliance was further manifested in her capacity to craft her own solutions, whether nurturing homegrown vegetables, creating her signature wines, weaving garments, designing bespoke jewelry, or adorning walls with her personalized paint strokes. The refrain of "can't" was unheard in her lexicon; instead, she danced through life on her toes, poised for any opportunity that beckoned.

Her educational voyage led her beyond the boundaries of her intimate town, exposing her to the diverse world of inner-city life. This encounter kindled in Leslie a profound respect for the myriad paths that humans tread, amplifying her empathy and understanding for all walks of life. Her journey also intertwined with the indefatigable energy of farmers, a spirit akin to the determined immigrants she now encounters within her English as a second language classes. As she witnesses their Herculean efforts, she finds echoes of the toil she observed on those expansive farmlands. Immigrants, much like those resilient tillers of the land, arrive on distant shores with nothing but a suitcase or backpack, weaving the threads of their life experiences and cultural heritage into the fabric of a new beginning.

The transition to a foreign land presents an arduous learning curve, particularly for adults navigating the labyrinth of language acquisition and cultural assimilation. The struggle to balance traditional family values with the nuances of a new society echoes the challenges Leslie observed as she traversed the hallways of her small-town school and encountered diverse worlds beyond. It's a testament to the strength of the human spirit, the unyielding resolve to carve a better life for oneself and one's progeny, to stand tall despite the odds.

Leslie's journey through small-town simplicity, urban complexity, and the resilient corridors of immigration weaves a ribbon of resilience, tenacity, and the belief that work ethic isn't just a concept, but a compass guiding one's pursuit of fulfillment and success, regardless of the setting or circumstance.

Business In A Small Town

Leslie saw that the small businesses in the town displayed a great work ethic because of the many hours that their employees worked to make a difference in the quality of their business. The workers were very personal and always willing to help the customers with orders and any customer service issues. There was no place for 'arrogance.' Their personality fits the hometown feel with a smile, nice body language, and welcoming language. Another trait that the workers carried was a sense of honesty with their service and the language that they displayed. If they presented a product or service to you that you returned later that was not up to the standards of quality, they would take it back with no issue. The employees were also friendly when you would meet them on the street and acted as if they were a part of your family.

This honesty in business dealing came from the community and how people were raised. The town was simple, but had people with good values. There was a sense of pride in one's work and the communication of the employees was a reflection of the contentedness of the people in the neighborhood because of the town being a strong church community. In the businesses, people showed extra energy because of really enjoying their business which was located among people in the town they felt comfortable with. The owners also lived nearby where they understood the people in the town because of being 'one of the same' with the same values.

Observing the workers in small businesses, made Leslie understand that all levels of society have a big contribution with their work ethic to the final result. These workers provide a significant path for the success of any business. They are not afraid to get their hands dirty.

At the time that Leslie lived in the community, there were no large superstores like Home Depot or

Giant Supermarket. As these chain stores replaced the small businesses, they took away the employees' pride and honor. The businesses care mostly about profits and the work ethic of their employees has been lost to some extent because of the management style and how the employees are treated. The workers may only be paid minimum wage with no benefits and be treated with a machine mentality. ('They may have an attitude because of a disregard for respecting them as human beings.') The employees then will only work a minimum in terms of their position and display limited energy because of not being rewarded. Employees will only go as far as they are treated, and not further.

The Farms

Leslie observed that the farms surrounding the neighborhood have a rich community with skilled labor and work ethic shown in every venture they get involved in. There are many Mennonites and Amish in the area that learn a new skill just to survive. They know the power of work! They have pride in what they accomplish and display honesty, and personalize every negotiation.

Growing up, Leslie visited the farms to buy produce which was a fun experience of picking out vegetables and fruits. She saw the hard labor on the farms as work ethic because of the 12 or 16-hour days, 7 days a week. These hours were necessary to take care of the animals, and the crops because they are harvested at a certain time. The area had only small farms with less than five family members that worked on each one. The profit was so slim that they could not afford to hire more people. Leslie's friend, Mary, lived on one of these farms and realized early on that she was not 'of that mold' because she didn't feel that it was the right fit. Mary later on became a doctor.

Leslie remembers the honesty and kindness of the farmers. They also taught the same values and work ethic to their children, and they were trained to assist the parents with the whole operation of the farm. Whatever business the Mennonites or Amish tackled, the children were always a part of the workforce. They had to grow up fast and be responsible at a young age. 'Doing what children do' was not as much a part of their agenda.

When Leslie was young the Mennonites would come to see her father as patients and would park in the driveway in the back of the house, where his private practice was located. Her father would also travel to their farmhouses to deliver babies because the Mennonites did not have medical insurance. She remembers how private and proper the old-order Mennonites were because of their religious life and not being used to the presence of other kinds of people. Joking was not part of their culture, at least in public.

Education: Reality vs Expectations

Private College - Albright College

At the age of 18, Leslie embarked on her journey at Albright College, nestled in the heart of Reading, Pennsylvania. Guided by her father's aspirations, she was set on the path to follow in his esteemed footsteps, envisaging a future as a medical doctor through a Pre-Med major. This familial aspiration had been instilled in her from a tender age, with her father's influence securing her admission to the very institution he once walked. The trajectory seemed inevitable, leaving Leslie with little room for alternative paths. Her academic pursuits were firmly anchored in medicine, and her father's steadfast support was contingent upon this sole course.

In the backdrop of Reading, an ancient city with a close-knit community, Leslie found herself immersed in an environment steeped in a robust work ethic. Despite the city's modest scale, pockets of industries persisted, providing labor positions for the hardworking denizens. This collective commitment to diligent labor was palpable, creating a backdrop where perseverance was a shared ethos.

Leslie discovered an undercurrent of this work ethic on her college campus as well. The surrounding community, cognizant of the vital role work plays in securing a prosperous life for their families, echoed this sentiment. The resonance of this shared dedication to toil resonated through the halls of Albright College, underscoring the importance of earnest effort in carving one's path.

Yet, after dedicating herself to Albright College for a year and a half, Leslie confronted a pivotal realization. The realm of chemistry, biology, and even the sight of blood, felt distant and detached from her essence. A metamorphosis was underway. With pragmatism and a newfound sense of self-awareness, Leslie discerned that a Business Major held a more fitting promise for her future. This transition in her academic pursuits led her to the embrace of Temple University in Philadelphia, Pennsylvania, a shift that aligned her studies more harmoniously with her innate inclinations.

.

Public University - Temple University

Transitioning to the realm of a public university was akin to stepping onto a whole new playing field. Here, a cornucopia of majors unfurled before Leslie, accompanied by a vibrant opportunity of campus events that added color to her collegiate experience. The work ethic pulsating through this environment bore a distinct character, divergent from her prior encounters. This public university was set against the backdrop of a lower socioeconomic area, a milieu where Leslie couldn't help but perceive a certain deficit in the prevailing work ethic of the society.

In an atmosphere riddled with struggle and challenges, it was not uncommon for a hint of waning motivation to seep into the fabric of the campus. This undertone occasionally manifested itself among certain students, reflecting the broader societal dynamics at play.

During Leslie's tenure at the university, an era of Open Enrollment beckoned, ushering in a diverse array of students representing varying degrees of preparedness and readiness. Alas, the journey was not without its obstacles, and a number of students found themselves succumbing to the tides of life's complexities, leading them to part ways with the institution.

The orbit of the university extended beyond its campus borders, casting a ripple of disconnection among the neighboring community members who felt somewhat excluded from its mission. Yet, for Leslie, the tapestry of diversity woven into the campus fabric was a constant source of fascination, ensuring that every moment was imbued with vitality and verve, thanks to the whirlwind of engaging events that unfolded within its precincts.

Public University - Grad School - West Chester University

During her graduate studies at a public university, Leslie's work ethic knew no bounds. The concept of saying 'no' to work was foreign to her. As she embarked on the journey of crafting research papers, Leslie faced the formidable challenge of grappling with a writing style she had little experience with. When Leslie claims to lack experience, it's no exaggeration.

While some of her peers would hunker down to write their papers just the weekend before they were due, Leslie found herself requiring more time. Often, she would embark on a complete rewrite, laboriously starting anew. Her dedication to refining her work knew no limits.

Fortuitously, her professor, who also served as her mentor for many of her courses, stood as a guiding light during this arduous process. Together, they forged a partnership, working side by side to tackle the daunting task of crafting these academic papers.

At the outset, Leslie's grasp of the fundamentals of writing left much to be desired. This prompted her to seek extensive guidance. One of her professors once advised, "Elevate your language register," which led Leslie to acquire a thesaurus. This newfound resource became akin to a sacred text, a constant companion on her academic journey. Prior to this, Leslie's writing style resembled casual conversation with a friend. With the thesaurus at her side, she embarked on a linguistic transformation, mining synonyms and integrating sophisticated vocabulary to infuse her work with newfound richness and eloquence.

Personal Interests: The Escape

Tennis - A Community

Leslie found solace and vitality in her adult tennis pursuits, fostering mental and physical well-being. Tennis demanded intense focus, leaving no space for distractions, as she often emphasized, "Stay alert and swift on the courts!"

Beyond personal gratification, tennis enriched Leslie's social life, aligning with her dedicated work ethic. Transforming it into a part-time endeavor, she orchestrated singles and doubles matches, engaging in multiple weekly sessions with diverse peers, participating in leagues and arrangements. Her resounding answer to tennis was an unhesitating,"Yes, yes, yes."

Leslie firmly believed that frequent play, a minimum of twice weekly, could propel anyone's skill level upward. Her 20-year dedication to five weekly sessions on hard courts yielded a formidable forehand, her friends attested. Confidence surged through consistent play, despite her non-athlete background; experience honed her prowess. Tennis became her constant muse.

Learning from diverse playing styles and shot velocities, Leslie engaged with men and women alike, gleaning insights. Adjustments became second nature; she learned to retreat slightly for slice shots, swiftly countering high, lofted balls with sharp-angled returns over the net. Execution, however, proved more intricate than theory.

In recent times, Leslie's enjoyment extended to pickleball, a leisurely pursuit in her view, offering a delightful departure from her rigorous tennis routine.

Jazz - More Than a Genre of Music

Leslie's fervor for jazz encompasses both immersive listening and piano performance. Honing her piano skills, she receives biweekly lessons from a distinguished jazz musician. A diligent practitioner, she carefully perfects newly acquired techniques. When tackling a fresh song, she studies YouTube performances, selecting a style that resonates, aspiring to emulate the essence while sculpting her unique interpretation.

Recently, Leslie embarked on the challenge of mimicking Bill Evans' rendition of "I Hear a Rhapsody," featuring powerful block chords. This intricate pursuit elevates her playing, albeit one phrase at a time, as mastering the complete piece demands a lifetime. Undaunted, incremental progress elates her momentarily, despite the occasional head-bumping frustration.

With her enduring work ethic, Leslie refines familiar pieces to incorporate newfound skills, imparting a professional flair. She often resets to square one, encountering head-scratching moments that test her perseverance.

Recording multiple video sessions, Leslie scrutinizes her piano performance, seeking perfection in half-hour segments. Imperfections are a reminder of humanity, prompting introspection and growth. Confident recordings are shared with her piano teacher and submitted to a London-based virtual piano meetup, an exhilarating experience amid grand piano virtuosos.

Currently, Leslie undertakes a novel endeavor—organizing a Facebook-based virtual piano meetup for intermediate players. This audacious project, initially for her teacher's students, may evolve into a broader community endeavor, driven by her unyielding motivation and spirit of experimentation.

Traveling The Globe

Leslie's explorations across the globe have acted as a gateway to profound insights, unraveling the intricate struggles faced by individuals hailing from developing nations, revealing the resolute manner in which they navigate the challenges of survival. Her footsteps graced the soils of Saudi Arabia, Morocco, India, and Vietnam, each destination unfurling a new chapter in her understanding.

Back within the borders of her homeland, the United States, Leslie's professional journey led her to forge connections with a diverse population of immigrants. These interactions provided her with a profound window into their unyielding work ethic, a trait they carry across oceans to their new abode. The narrative of most immigrants begins from the very foundation—starting anew, embracing a life of tireless effort to master a foreign language, undertaking humble jobs, and attending to basic needs. No task is beneath them, whether it entails delivering pizzas or tending to the upkeep of households. They stand unflinching, their hands unafraid to embrace the grittier aspects of life.

The beauty of Leslie's vantage point lies in her appreciation for the aspirations of immigrants, who labor tirelessly to bestow their progeny with the prospect of a brighter tomorrow. They embrace a plethora of employments, unafraid to dedicate 10 or even 12 hours a day, seven days a week, to provide for their kin. As Leslie encounters fresh faces within her English as a Second Language classes, she imparts sagely advice–a roadmap to prosperity that involves cultivating a venture where one's contributions are valued. Their untiring dedication, culminating in hours upon hours of labor, promises the fruition of success within their own enterprise, if circumstance permits. Alternatively, they might find themselves toiling in factories, eateries, or pizza joints, settings that may offer subpar working conditions and potentially subject them to language and education-based discrimination. The challenges they encounter span a spectrum–nonpayment, protracted hours, an absence of benefits, and the dark cloud of harassment.

Beyond the confines of the United States, Leslie's expeditions have infused her with profound appreciation, akin to the feeling she experiences when she gazes out from the windows of a taxi and beholds immigrants, adorned with advanced degrees, embroiled in labor-intensive pursuits. Their diligence, she realizes, is a manifestation of their aspiration to foster a brighter tomorrow for their offspring. These immigrant children stand tall with towering aspirations–dreams of majoring in economics, computer science, or other scientific disciplines. Eagerly, they embrace the value of hard work, unafraid to weave its threads into the fabric of their existence. The truth of the matter is apparent–those arriving from foreign lands are not beneficiaries of a "free ride."

The world of global exploration has provided an invaluable lesson into Leslie's outlook–a reverence for the fruits of her labor and a discerning approach to consumption. The connection between toil and reward has underscored the wisdom of not squandering resources frivolously, prompting a conscious choice to procure only that which is truly essential. The realization has dawned that the effort poured into endeavors serves as a guiding compass, guiding prudent choices and encouraging a perspective that values substance over excess.

Morocco

Morocco enticed Leslie, captivating her senses with its unique allure. Among the many captivating corners, one stood out as an absolute gem–the ancient city of Fez, a veritable portal to a bygone era. This timeless enclave, meticulously preserved across the expanse of centuries, beckons visitors to traverse its labyrinthine streets and peer into the annals of history.

Fez, the jewel in Morocco's crown, bears witness to a fascinating juxtaposition of eras. As modernity strides forward, the old city remains an unyielding bastion, frozen in time. Venturing through its hallowed streets, one encounters an entrancing scene—a symphony of merchants and their steadfast donkeys gracefully navigating narrow thoroughfares, while inquisitive tourists step aside, their senses ablaze with the sights and sounds of a living tableau.

The very fabric of the old city unfurls before the observer, a tightly woven frame work of cement structures that house vibrant markets, tranquil churches, bustling schools, and the heartbeat of local life—the residences. Here, a unique decree reigns—no vehicles breach these hallowed precincts. Instead, it is the artisans who claim dominion, their spaces upon the cement ground transforming into an open-air theater of creation. Before the very eyes of intrigued onlookers, they craft their wares, each motion a dance of devotion, each product a testament to their unyielding pride.

In every artisan's creation, there is an unspoken pledge—an unyielding commitment to excellence, a pledge woven into the very fabric of Fez's identity. Leslie's discerning eyes bear witness to this commitment, noting that the products that spring forth from these skilled hands are nothing short of exceptional. Quality, unmatched and unrivaled, saturates every creation, and it's a quality that remains etched in Leslie's memory like an indelible mark.

As Leslie reflects on her journey through the time-honored streets of Fez, she carries with her a memento more enduring than any physical souvenir—a piece of this ancient city, forever embedded in the recesses of her heart. The echoes of Fez's bustling markets, the artisans' pride, and the timeless charm of its unchanged visage will continue to reverberate through her thoughts, a cherished connection that time cannot erode.

Japan

While Leslie has personally visited Japan, a lot of her information has come from her brother Todd who worked for many years for a Japanese company and visited Japan many times.

In Japan, people work for many hours a day and work at the same company for many years. This is expected of them. As a result of this work ethic, the products and services of Japanese companies are superior because of the pride of the employees.

It is said by many that the quality of the products is better than the other Asian countries, and a lot of other countries. A prime example of the Japanese work ethic is that it is not uncommon that some workers are at their job so late that they miss their last train home at midnight, and thus have to stay outside the station till the next morning.

Saudi Arabia

In 1973, Leslie traveled to Saudi Arabia and lived with an American family in an American compound. She stayed there for six weeks and learned how work ethic plays a big part in Saudi's life. At that time she observed that people had a lot of small businesses to survive and worked many hours a day.

Some of the companies that Leslie encountered were Thobe stores, where traditional dress for men and women is sold, Arab bread stores, the gold market, where jewelers produced their gold pieces and sandals stores, where they made sandals from camel spit and leather.

One can also work for an oil company and make it big, but not everyone is an engineer or doctor. The oil is a big business in Saudi Arabia; as a result, the country has become 'very rich.' In the 1970s, the oil companies started increasing its production, and there were a lot of people starting to increase their income because of this situation. ('Oil makes you powerful.')

There were also people from other developing countries that were employed to work on people's houses and gardens. They cleaned their houses, and worked in their garden every day. They made sure that the areas that they cleaned were spotless because they could not afford to lose their job, due to the fact that they sent all the money back to their family in their native country. They worked ten months out of the year and went back to their country for two months to see their family. The house and garden boys had the dedication to their family. Leslie had never seen this before. How can there be more dedication to one's family?

The Work Ethic of People in Varied Businesses

In the realm of a rubber stamp manufacturer, Leslie specialized in distributing pre-inked stamps that provided a convenient marking solution until the ink depletion, warranting an easy replacement. Within two years or sooner, Leslie orchestrated the seamless transition to a new marking device. With vigor, she embarked on a daily regimen of 50 assertive cold calls, building a robust clientele that anticipated her visits every few months. Humorously, she adopted the moniker 'Stamp Lady,' eliciting chuckles from the business folk.

Leslie's robust work ethic shone through her adeptness at sealing the deal through five strategic interactions per call. Each rejection propelled her to navigate conversations with determination, culminating in successful transactions with managers. Proficient in devising specialized applications, she deftly demonstrated physical samples or swiftly conceptualized tailored solutions on-site.

Her prowess earned Leslie the distinction of being the premier salesperson in Philadelphia for an impressive 13-year span, ranking among the country's top sales representatives. Echoing her impact, the national sales manager wistfully remarked, 'I wish I could clone more Leslies.'

Food Stand at Farmer's Market

Leslie observes the Amish workforce, a harmonious blend of youth and experience, embodying a resolute work ethic that encompasses every facet of their enterprise—quite literally, from A to Z. These diligent workers orchestrate the creation of delectable pies, cakes, and cookies, a symphony of culinary craftsmanship destined for distant urban markets. Undaunted by hours of travel, they collectively contribute to the entire process: crafting, transporting, stocking, and attending to customers with utmost care.

For the Amish, work is a sacred commitment instilled from an early age, a principle that fuels their dedication to ten- and twelve-hour workdays. Their concept of time is fluid, shaped by the organic rhythm of the task at hand, rather than the confines of a clock. Rooted in generations of Amish heritage, they understand that their labor demands tireless energy, unencumbered by rigid schedules—a way of life that brooks no alternative, compelling adherence to established norms.

Amish households offer scant leisure for their young occupants, as family businesses beckon from an early stage. Yet, despite their labor-intensive responsibilities, the Amish emanate a genuine and affable demeanor, driven by their simple upbringing and ingrained respect for authority. With minimal conflict marring their work environment, they readily extend assistance to inquiries, embodying a service-oriented ethos alongside their product offerings.

The Amish grasp that service and quality are inseparable companions in their trade. A sense of duty compels them to deliver nothing short of excellence, an ethos underscored by their unrelenting commitment to perfection. Their efforts transcend the realm of mere transactions, embodying a profound dedication to producing superlative results.

Biologist in a Laboratory

Leslie observes the biologist within the laboratory, captivated by the profound dedication that underpins their pursuit of a vaccine. The scientist's unshakable commitment to unraveling a medical enigma is nothing short of inspiring. Driven by an ardent passion for alleviating human suffering, they immerse themselves in the intricate process with a fervor that borders on devotion.

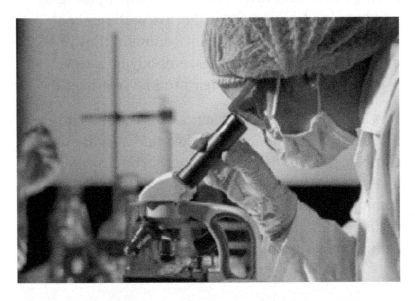

The biologist's resolute focus on their field of study is unmistakable, and their unyielding dedication transforms into a wellspring of tireless effort. Pouring every ounce of energy into unraveling the complex puzzle before them, they embark on a journey fueled by genuine curiosity and compassion. Theirs is a mission to offer aid to those in dire need, a noble purpose that fuels their relentless pursuit of a breakthrough.

As each milestone is achieved and a solution materializes, the scientist's spirit is reignited, setting ablaze a beacon of motivation for future endeavors. This triumph becomes a testament to their work ethic, driving them to continue forging new paths and devising innovative solutions to intricate medical challenges. The biologist's quest is not merely a scientific pursuit; it's a testament to the staunch commitment of a dedicated soul on a mission to reshape the future of healthcare.

Construction Workers From Other Countries

Leslie keenly observes the construction workers hailing from diverse corners of the globe, toiling diligently on houses and construction sites. Their exceptional work ethic resonates deeply, driven by a profound sense of gratitude for the opportunity to earn a living in a land where wages surpass those of their homeland.

Amidst the clang of tools and the bustle of the site, their tireless energy and dedication stand out. These individuals exude a sense of purpose and commitment, embracing their roles with humility and a steadfast adherence to the directives of their supervisors. Their punctuality and unflagging presence further exemplify their dedication.

These workers exhibit a remarkable level of determination, embodying the very essence of the phrase "whatever it takes." Their motivation springs from the promise of a better existence, a chance to inhabit a more prosperous nation and forge a brighter future for themselves and their families. Their presence is a testament to the enduring human spirit and the aspiration for a life enriched by new opportunities.

Local Bartender

Leslie has observed the local bartender exemplifying a commendable work ethic, ensuring that each customer receives their requested drink promptly and without pressure. With a keen sense of timing, the bartender artfully presents his offerings, allowing patrons to enjoy their experience at their own pace.

In addition to his efficient service, the bartender demonstrates a commitment to cleanliness and professionalism. Regularly tending to the bar area and meticulously cleaning glassware and utensils, he underscores his dedication to upholding a polished and welcoming ambiance.

Skillfully engaging in meaningful conversations, the bartender tailors his interactions to suit the clientele, fostering a sense of ease and comfort. His professionalism shines through in every interaction, reflecting his dedication to representing the establishment in the best possible light. Averse to negativity, he upholds the standards of good business, ensuring a positive and inviting environment for all patrons.

Furthermore, the bartender adeptly maintains order and decorum, swiftly handling any unruly situations that may arise, thus contributing to the establishment's overall professional and inviting atmosphere.

Local Dry Cleaners

Leslie noticed that the dry cleaner business, owned by the same individuals for a span of 15 years, stands as a testament to their unremitting commitment to excellence. Not only do they impeccably clean garments, but they also skillfully undertake minor clothing repairs. Leslie has had the privilege of witnessing their consistent delivery of outstanding service to the local community. Their dry cleaning services exude quality, and their interactions with customers are marked by warmth and genuine care.

With a friendly demeanor, the owners excel at engaging in meaningful small talk, fostering a sense of connection and rapport. Their dedication to customer satisfaction knows no bounds - they readily go the extra mile to ensure the happiness of every patron. Recognizing the demands of the neighborhood, they operate tirelessly six days a week, investing long hours that reflect their commitment to thriving in today's economy. Their business is not merely a venture but a way of life, characterized by diligence and a strong work ethic that leaves no room for complacency.

As the owners contemplate departing from the business, Leslie anticipates missing their presence dearly, for their genuine dedication and exceptional service have left an indelible mark on the community.

Owner, Local Bagel Restaurant

Leslie realized that Hudah and her family epitomize the essence of hard work, having recently immigrated to the United States from Syria and Iraq. Their journey is rooted in the need to provide for their family's well-being. Hudah, a former attorney in Iraq, and her husband, who owned a pickle factory, embarked on a year-long endeavor to establish a bagel/Middle Eastern restaurant. Their dedication culminated in the restaurant's grand opening in August 2022.

Prior to launching their own establishment, Hudah honed her culinary skills by working at a bagel restaurant across the street, mastering the art of crafting bagels from scratch. Armed with this expertise, she seamlessly integrated it into her new venture, crafting delectable bagels in the morning and a fusion of Middle Eastern and other cultural cuisines in the afternoon and early evening, with a particular emphasis on Middle Eastern fare.

Hudah's commitment to her work is resoundingly evident as she commences her day at an early 3 am, diligently preparing fresh bagels from scratch. The restaurant opens its doors at 6 am and extends its service until 6 pm, operating seven days a week. With a keen understanding of their diverse clientele, Hudah ensures the highest quality of bagels, a staple that attracts patrons from all walks of life. Her generosity shines through as she offers complimentary bagels to children.

The familial synergy is palpable within the restaurant's bustling ambiance. Hudah and her husband expertly execute their roles, both in the kitchen and with dishwashing duties, while their daughter adeptly handles orders, payments, and service. Their commitment to providing made-to-order meals infuses an atmosphere of freshness and quality.

The enormity of the task at hand doesn't deter Hudah and her husband; they draw from their prior restaurant ownership experience to navigate the demands. Their unparalleled work ethic is further amplified by their profound responsibility to support their family, consisting of four remarkable daughters who are pursuing high school and college education.

Hudah's dedication extends beyond the restaurant's walls. She generously bestows me with a variety of bagels, complemented by cream cheese that exudes flavors reminiscent of cheesecake. Hudah's pursuit of excellence is resolute, a testament to her unrelenting commitment to being the best in her field.

Local Food Store

Leslie keenly observes the food store's employees exemplifying a commendable work ethic, which is evidently fostered by the favorable working environment they enjoy. Their confidence in the superior quality of the food they offer radiates throughout their interactions with customers. The exceptional service they provide, coupled with the excellence of their products, creates a magnetism that draws repeat customers who wholeheartedly place their trust in the business's mission and values.

Owner, Local Diner

Affectionately known as 'Little Pete' due to his stature, Leslie experienced that the owner defies any notions of 'short service' or 'short quality.' His unparalleled work ethic sets him apart as a remarkable restaurateur, leaving a lasting impression on Leslie. Hailing from Greece, Pete has masterfully transformed the diner into a culinary gem, boasting impeccable service and exceptional cuisine.

Little Pete's culinary repertoire is as diverse as it is impressive. Whether it's delectable Greek, Italian, or Jewish dishes, his menu is a tantalizing journey of flavors. Portion sizes are generous, and every dinner is a delightful ensemble complete with soup, salad, bread, dessert, and a beverage. A true embodiment of dedication, Pete takes on various roles within the diner - from cooking to table-setting, clearing, and hosting. He's always engaged in making customers' experiences exceptional; no task is beneath him.

Service is paramount within the establishment, a reflection of the high standards set by Pete. Residents of the building have come to expect top-tier service and quality cuisine, and Pete delivers on both fronts. He nurtures a warm and familial ambiance, engaging in heartfelt conversations that make patrons feel like cherished members of the extended diner family. This personal touch transforms mere visitors into loyal regulars, transcending backgrounds and incomes.

In the wake of the pandemic, Pete has faced challenges in staffing his kitchen. Undeterred, he rises to the occasion, often donning his apron at the early hour of 3 AM to prepare meals himself. It's a testament to his unshakeable commitment and passion for his craft.

For Leslie and her husband, dining at Little Pete's restaurant is not just about the delectable dishes; it's a reunion with a dear friend. Familiar faces abound, both from their building and the broader neighborhood, evoking a sense of belonging and camaraderie. Stepping into the restaurant feels like coming home, where every guest is treated like family.

Work Ethic in Academia and Community Service

Friend, a Professor

During the previous semester, when Leslie stepped into the professor's classroom, she was truly captivated by the professor's unwavering passion for teaching. The whiteboards were brimming with meticulously detailed assignments and essential dates, showcasing the professor's exceptional work ethic. Prior to the commencement of each class, the professor would dedicate time to personally engage with students at the back of the room, offering guidance on their writing endeavors.

As the class commenced, the professor consistently distributed helpful handouts, a practice that left Leslie wondering if such dedicated teaching persists in today's world. The professor's instruction was rich with valuable insights, conveyed with an air of tranquility that underscored her genuine commitment to nurturing English as a second language students.

Leslie was also deeply touched by the professor's courteous manner. Notably, the professor took a moment to commend Leslie's presentation on the Learning Lab, displaying a generosity that reflected her sincere interest in both individuals and her profession. It's these small yet impactful gestures that set this professor apart—a true exemplar of kindness and dedication, leaving a lasting impression on all fortunate enough to be her students. Indeed, her students proudly declare, "There is no one quite like this exceptional professor."

Professor Number Two

At the local college where Leslie teaches, there is a remarkable professor who serves as a colleague and source of support. While not in a supervisory role, this professor's enduring availability and responsiveness have left a lasting impression on Leslie. Whenever Leslie reaches out via email or phone, the professor's immediate and willing assistance shines through, setting her apart from others in the department.

What truly distinguishes this professor is her exceptional work ethic, which stems from a genuine passion for excellence and a profound care for others. Her involvement in various committees and contributions to the English as a second language department reflect her commitment to both her profession and her colleagues. Despite her busy schedule, the professor maintains an uplifting outlook on life and consistently extends her assistance beyond the confines of her job description.

This professor's actions speak volumes about her character and dedication. Her willingness to support students, faculty, and colleagues alike has made a lasting impact on those fortunate enough to cross her path. Leslie is grateful for the privilege of knowing such an extraordinary individual and realizes that encounters with someone of this caliber are rare indeed. This professor's exceptional qualities and contributions truly make her a standout figure at the college.

College Supervisor

Leslie's supervisor at the college is an exemplary individual who not only excels in her job but also exudes genuine care and compassion. Her prompt responsiveness and provision of valuable information showcase her dedication to serving others effectively. This supervisor's commendable work ethic is a testament to her holistic attitude toward people and her never-failing passion for her responsibilities.

On multiple occasions, Leslie has witnessed this supervisor's remarkable empathy firsthand. Even when faced with challenges not directly related to her own students, such as a student's hospitalization or a family crisis, the supervisor expresses heartfelt concern. This genuine compassion creates a deep connection and resonates with students, showcasing the supervisor's exceptional commitment to their well-being.

This supervisor's unique combination of empathy and professionalism makes her particularly well-suited for overseeing returning adult students who may be navigating personal instability. Her evident passion for uplifting others and her sincere investment in their success contribute significantly to her effectiveness as a supervisor. Leslie is genuinely inspired by her supervisor's dedication and feels privileged to work under the guidance of such an outstanding role model.

Supervisor at a Non-Profit

Leslie had the privilege of observing her supervisor's remarkable leadership as the head of a local non-profit organization over the course of many years. This dedicated individual embodies an exceptional work ethic that is truly awe-inspiring. The organization itself is a beacon of support, offering a comprehensive range of vital services including English language assistance, GED programs, tax preparation, Covid vaccinations, housing guidance, mental health support, and after-school initiatives.

Remarkably, her journey with this organization began during her high school years when she selflessly volunteered her time. Through unflappable dedication and commitment, she steadily climbed the ranks to eventually assume the role of Executive Director, a position she has expertly held for the past two decades.

Motivated by her own background, having started in a modest household and later transitioning to a suburban setting, this dynamic woman channels her boundless energy into running the agency. Her passion is deeply rooted in her empathy for the clients, many of whom face challenging poverty-related circumstances. Having experienced similar hardships herself, she extends her guidance and support to her colleagues who may be navigating comparable difficulties. Her genuine desire to make a positive impact on the lives of those in need is evident in every aspect of her work.

Beyond her role, she has a particular affinity for serving the segment of society she identifies with, including her own Vietnamese community. This intrinsic connection and understanding render her an ideal fit for the organization's mission and values.

Leslie is truly inspired by her supervisor's tireless commitment and heartfelt dedication, and she remains fortunate to have had the opportunity to witness such an exceptional leader in action.

Witnessing Students' Work Ethics

Student Interactions

In the class that Leslie instructs, a commendable group of students consistently exemplifies a strong and dedicated work ethic. Their commitment to their education is evident through their punctuality, attending all sessions without fail. Moreover, they approach assignments with persistent determination, investing an impressive '150% energy' to ensure timely completion and exceptional quality.

These diligent students embrace their coursework with enthusiasm, consistently delivering their best effort on homework and actively engaging in classroom discussions. Their participation not only enriches the learning environment but also underscores their commitment to the subject matter.

In addition to their academic dedication, these students exhibit a profound respect for their instructor and their fellow classmates. They display this respect by raising their hands to seek clarification and responding attentively when addressed by the teacher. Should circumstances arise that prevent their attendance or promptness, they proactively communicate with the instructor well in advance.

Remarkably mature, these students recognize and embrace their roles as dedicated learners, prioritizing their studies above all else. Their single-minded focus on academic excellence is a testament to their strong sense of responsibility and commitment to achieving favorable outcomes.

A Determined Student, Non-Profit

One student's remarkable work ethic has deeply impressed Leslie. In 2012, this determined individual left El Salvador and embarked on a journey to the United States. Seeking assistance with English as a second language, she turned to a local non-profit organization after already earning a Bachelor's degree in Biology in her home country. Her dedication was evident as she transitioned from the non-profit to enroll in a local community college, achieving two Associate Degrees before successfully completing a

Bachelor's Degree at a prestigious college. Her thirst for knowledge remained unquenchable as she went on to earn a Master's Degree in Forensic Science from a well-regarded university. Her boundless energy and tenacity are truly remarkable.

    The student's exceptional work ethic stems from the challenges she has faced since arriving in the country, compounded by her family situation. Raised by her grandmother in El Salvador, she arrived in the United States at the age of 19 to join her mother and father, who had immigrated when she was a child. Despite her parents' divorce and the unique dynamic of their relationship, resembling more of siblings than traditional parents, she has maintained a positive attitude and pleasant demeanor. Her surroundings, though in a lower socio-economic neighborhood, have only fueled her determination to pursue education despite adversity, maintaining an unfaltering motivation even in the face of challenges.

    Her commitment to her education has led her to a promising career at a pharmaceutical company. Recently becoming a mother to a baby girl named Bella, she is fiercely dedicated to providing for her daughter's future and ensuring a stable family environment. Leslie has been lending her support through a non-profit organization to help the student navigate her journey and seek assistance from the father of her child, showcasing the student's incredible attitude towards life's situations.

In every way, this individual stands as a shining example of resilience, perseverance, and determination. Her story is a testament to the power of a strong work ethic and an unbreakable spirit.

Special Student

In Leslie's Listening/Speaking English as a second language class, there was a remarkable student who stood out for her exceptional work ethic and dedication to assignments. This student's commitment shone through as she consistently went above and beyond, providing extensive additional information for exercises and investing long hours into completing her work. Beyond her individual efforts, she also displayed a genuine concern for her fellow students, taking the initiative to share valuable insights on topics like financial aid and banking information.

What truly sets this student apart is her outstanding attitude, which undoubtedly will contribute to her success in various aspects of life. It is evident that her strong work ethic will seamlessly transition into a professional setting, where she will undoubtedly go the extra mile and make significant contributions to any organization she becomes a part of. Her unique qualities make her a standout individual, and her future accomplishments are bound to make both her and her chosen company incredibly proud.

Incorporating Work Ethic In The Real World

When embarking on your professional journey, Leslie advises to explore diverse roles to gain a comprehensive understanding of the working world. Prioritize fair compensation for your efforts and recognition for your innovative ideas. Cultivating a mindset that goes beyond conventions will prove invaluable in your career. This could encompass roles within the non-profit sector, corporate realm, and small business landscape.

Engaging with a non-profit organization offers insight into how such entities aid others through grant acquisition and fundraising efforts. It provides valuable lessons in resourcefulness and surviving in dynamic environments, often catering to a base clientele facing instability.

Within the corporate sphere, financial gains drive decisions, and employees are seen as tools to achieve outcomes. Vigilance is crucial, as minor missteps can lead to swift termination in pursuit of enhanced profits. To safeguard your position, a diligent work ethic is essential, fostering quality outcomes that justify your role within the company.

Nurturing your career requires networking and staying current through attendance at conferences and workshops. This engagement not only enhances your credentials but also garners respect within your field. Staying attuned to emerging trends empowers you to contribute significantly to your organization. Cultivate professional relationships with colleagues both within and beyond your workplace. Recognize them not only as friends but as valuable connections striving for advancement. Strengthening ties on a professional level can open doors to external opportunities, ultimately enhancing your prospects for a fulfilling life journey.

About the Author

Leslie Killian Greenlee, M.A. (she/her/hers)

In 2012, after completing her Master's Degree in TESL (M.A.) from West Chester University, Leslie embarked on a rewarding journey as an instructor of English as a second language. Her academic foundation includes a Bachelor's Degree (B.A.) in Business Administration from Temple University.

With a 15-year tenure, Leslie has imparted her expertise at various esteemed institutions across Philadelphia. Her passion for education led her to positions in colleges, English language institutes, and a prominent non-profit organization. Her current role finds her dedicatedly shaping minds at the Community College of Philadelphia (CCP) for the past 6 years.

At CCP, Leslie skillfully imparts knowledge in Listening/Speaking and Reading/Writing, along with conducting insightful workshops and labs at the Learning Lab. Her contributions extend beyond the classroom, as she actively participates in the Course Learning Objectives Committee and Pay Equity Committee. Beyond the college, Leslie's commitment shines as she serves on the board for the Penn TESL East organization.

Leslie's global outreach includes teaching English teaching methods to Chinese educators in Nanjing, China, during 2012 and 2013. Her love for exploration has taken her to diverse corners of the world, from India and Morocco to Saudi Arabia, Japan, China, England, Poland, and beyond.

When not shaping minds, Leslie indulges in her passions. Swimming, playing jazz piano, tennis, and pickelball occupy her precious moments of leisure, showcasing her vibrant spirit outside the classroom.

Made in the USA
Middletown, DE
09 September 2023

37862491R10050